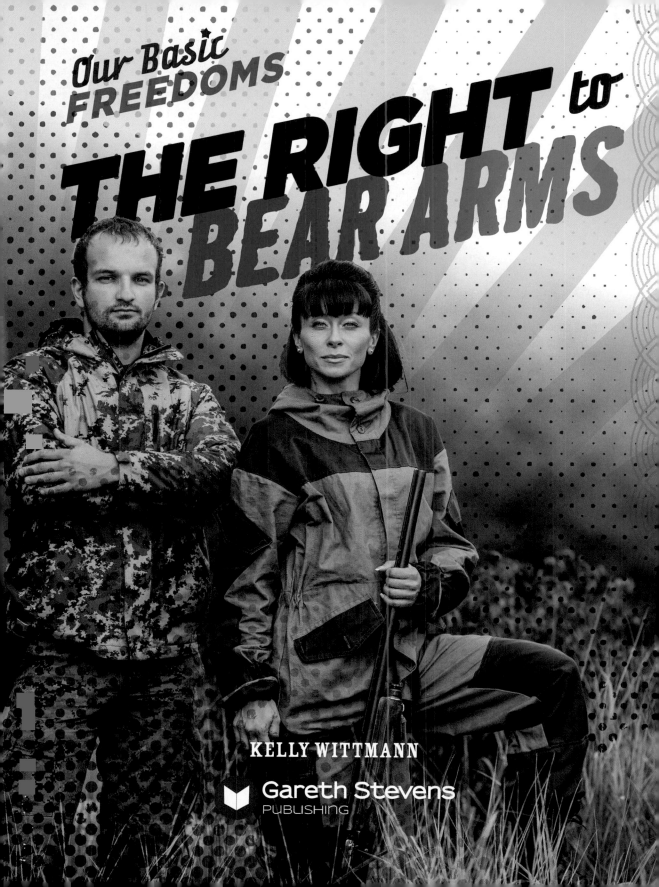

Our Basic
FREEDOMS

THE RIGHT to BEAR ARMS

KELLY WITTMANN

Gareth Stevens
PUBLISHING

Please visit our website, www.garethstevens.com.
For a free color catalog of all our high-quality books,
call toll free 1-800-542-2595 or fax 1-877-542-2596.

Cataloging-in-Publication Data

Names: Wittmann, Kelly.
Title: The right to bear arms / Kelly Wittmann.
Description: New York : Gareth Stevens Publishing, 2017. | Series: Our basic freedoms | Includes index.
Identifiers: ISBN 9781482461121 (pbk.) | ISBN 9781482461909 (library bound) | ISBN 9781482461138 (6 pack)
Subjects: LCSH: United States. Constitution. 2nd Amendment--Juvenile literature. | Firearms--Law and
  legislation--United States--Juvenile literature. | Gun control--United States--Juvenile literature.
Classification: LCC KF3941.W57 2017 | DDC 344.7305'33--dc23

Published in 2017 by
Gareth Stevens Publishing
111 East 14th Street, Suite 349
New York, NY 10003

Copyright © 2017 Gareth Stevens Publishing

Developed and Produced by Focus Strategic Communications, Inc.
Project Manager: Adrianna Edwards
Editor: Ron Edwards
Layout and Composition: Laura Brady, Ruth Dwight
Copyeditors: Adrianna Edwards, Francine Geraci
Media Researchers: Maria DeCambra, Adrianna Edwards
Proofreader: Francine Geraci
Index: Ron Edwards

Photo Credits: Credit Abbreviations: LOC Library of Congress; NARA National Archives and Records
Administration; S Shutterstock; WC Wikimedia Commons. Position on the page: T: top, C: center, B: bottom,
L: left, R: right. Cover: C: NEstudio/S; 4 T: Lori Martin/S; 4 B: Dean Drobot/S; 5: Daderot/WC; 6: Everett -
Art/S; 7: Everett Historical/S; 8: Everett Historical/S; 9: LOC/LC-USZC4-3362; 10: Vkilikov/S; 11: Everett
Historical/S; 12: Boston Public Library/Cab.25.58.1; 13: JPL Designs/S; 14: LOC/HABS VA, 30-LORT, 1-74; 15:
Annals of the King's Chapel from the Puritan Age of New England to the present day, by Foote et al., Boston:
Little, Brown, and Co., 1882. Digitized by the Princeton Theological Seminary Library; 16: Everett - Art/S; 17:
Antique Military Rifles/Flickr; 18: Everett Historical/S; 19: WC; 20: Everett Historical/S; 21: B Brown/S; 22:
Keith Homan/S; 23: jcjgphotography/S; 24: Koya979/S; 25: patrimonio designs ltd/S; 26: digitalreflections/S; 27:
Ververidis Vasilis/S; 28: Jeff Kern/WC; 29: Ron Frank/S; 30: Icedmocha/S; 33: Federal Bureau of Investigation;
34: Anatoly Vartanov/S; 35: Fer Gregory/S; 36: Yuliyan Velchev/S; 37: scottlitt/S; 38: Maksym Dykha/S; 39:
Mi.Ti./S; 40: MCarper/S; 41: Sergey Nivens/S; 42: somsak suwanput/S; 43: Lukas Gojda/S; 44: NICHOLAS
KAMM/Staff/Getty; 45: Tab62/S.

Printed in the United States of America
CPSIA compliance information: Batch CW17GS: For further information contact
Gareth Stevens, New York, New York at 1-800-542-2595.

CONTENTS

CHAPTER 1
MAKING OUR LIBERTIES CLEAR

A QUESTION OF RIGHTS

We, as Americans, have the right to bear arms because of the Second Amendment to the Bill of Rights. But what is the Bill of Rights? And why was the Second Amendment included in it?

Fast Fact

RIGHT TO BEAR ARMS OR BARE ARMS?

You have no doubt seen humorous photos of buff people (who seem to have just come from a workout) wearing a T-shirt or tank top with the slogan: "Right to Bare Arms." The joke, of course, is the play on the words "bear" and "bare." Both words sound the same but mean different things. James Madison and his pals were probably not talking about biceps and triceps when they composed the Second Amendment!

CONSTITUTIONAL CRISIS

The United States Constitution was created on September 17, 1787, and **ratified** on June 21, 1788. The Constitution was an important document because it represented the first time in world history that a government was established by democratically elected representatives of the common people. It was a great leap forward for the rights of humankind.

The US Constitution was signed in 1787 at the Constitutional Convention in Philadelphia.

GOVERNMENT AND RIGHTS

Still, not all representatives in the Continental Congress—or Founding Fathers, as we now call them—were satisfied with the Constitution. This subgroup of men was known as the **Anti-Federalists**. They were very concerned that if a centralized government had too much control over the states, America could return to some form of a **monarchy**. Not all Anti-Federalists opposed the Constitution altogether, but they all felt it did not go far enough in its protection of the rights of states and individual citizens. Once it was ratified, they all wanted to amend it.

Fast Fact

FOUNDING FATHERS

The men (yes, they were all guys) who debated and helped develop the document that defined the new country, the Constitution of the United States, are often called Founders—although who counts as a Founder depends on who you talk to. There is general agreement about the "Big Seven": John Adams, Benjamin Franklin (pictured here), Alexander Hamilton, Thomas Jefferson, James Madison, John Jay, and George Washington.

A NECESSARY COMPROMISE

Though some states quickly ratified the Constitution, others lagged behind as they argued for the rights of individuals. In Rhode Island, the opposition to the Constitution was so strong that its citizens threatened civil war. The representatives to the Continental Congress knew that some compromise had to made with Anti-Federalist supporters. James Madison, from Virginia, led the effort to bring these two groups to an agreement.

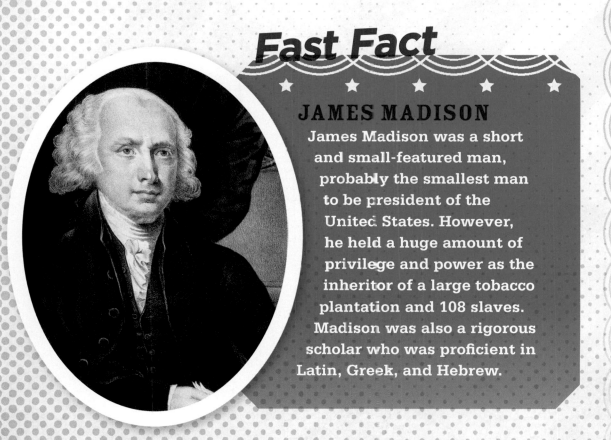

Fast Fact

JAMES MADISON

James Madison was a short and small-featured man, probably the smallest man to be president of the United States. However, he held a huge amount of privilege and power as the inheritor of a large tobacco plantation and 108 slaves. Madison was also a rigorous scholar who was proficient in Latin, Greek, and Hebrew.

COMPROMISE

The compromise with the Anti-Federalists was 10 **amendments** to the Constitution, which became known as the Bill of Rights. The Bill of Rights was written in New York City in 1789 and ratified in 1791. James Madison was known from that point on as "the Father of the Bill of Rights."

Fast Fact

★ ★ ★ ★

GEORGE MASON

The Bill of Rights was heavily influenced by the Virginia Declaration of Rights, which was written in 1776 by George Mason. Mason was later one of his state's delegates to the Constitutional Convention. Yet in the end, he (along with two other delegates) refused to sign the document because it lacked a bill of rights.

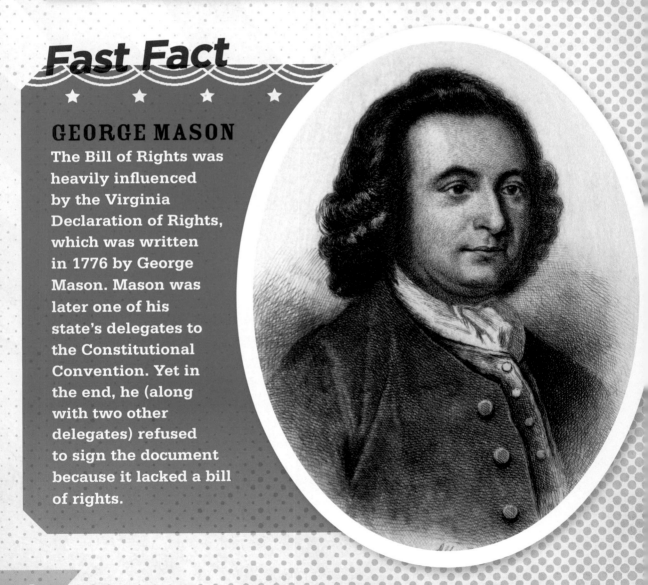

AMATEUR MILITIAS

The Second Amendment to the Bill of Rights is short and to the point: "A well-regulated **militia** being necessary to the security of a free state, the right of the people to keep and bear arms shall not be infringed." Unlike some other amendments (for example, the First Amendment), it does not cover a collection of rights, but one right only. The Founding Fathers seemed to want to set it apart in order to highlight its importance.

The Founders were proud of the role their citizen soldiers played in defeating the professional British army. They revered Washington and his military leadership that won the day, but they distrusted standing armies because of their experiences against the British. For example, James Madison repeatedly warned about the "tyranny" of armies and how they had "enslaved the people." Samuel Adams cautioned that a professional army was "always dangerous to the liberties of the people."

The Founding Fathers revered George Washington and his leadership during the war, but they never forgot the important role of the militia of citizen soldiers: the "minutemen" became a symbol of American determination.

FUTURE PROBLEMS

One would think that these warnings against professional armies would make the Second Amendment one of the most simple and understandable ideas in our founding documents. But the Founders could never have guessed the confusion and controversy that this one amendment would cause for generations to come.

The drafting of the Declaration of Independence is an iconic image, based on the John Trumbull portrait of 1819 (not to be confused with the signing of the famous document, which took place later). This image has appeared on the back of the US $2 bill since 1976.

WHO ARE "THE PEOPLE"?

Whether between Constitutional scholars or everyday Americans, the intellectual battles over the Second Amendment never seem to end. What is a "militia"? Who are "the people"? Are "the people" referred to collectively, or as individuals? And who gets to decide the answers to these questions—the legislative branch of the government (the Senate and House)? The judicial branch (the US court system)? Or the executive branch (the president of the United States and the Cabinet)?

Fast Fact

THE BILL OF RIGHTS: NOT FOR EVERYONE

The Bill of Rights did not apply to African Americans, whether slaves or free, even though they made up about 20 percent of the population around the time of the Revolutionary War. But many white Americans who had argued for their own freedom from England did begin to look at slavery with a more critical eye. The movement that grew out of this new consciousness was called **abolitionism**.

THE THREE BRANCHES OF GOVERNMENT

The United States established three branches of government so that no one branch would ever overpower the others. Our system is set up to have checks and balances intended to keep the nation on an even keel and benefit the many rather than the few. But some issues have proven to be a continual thorn in the side of the American public, and the Second Amendment is definitely one of those issues.

US POPULATION IN 1776

In 1776, about 25,000 people lived in New York City, the birthplace of the Bill of Rights. Philadelphia was the largest city in the colonies, with a population of about 40,000. Boston (pictured here) had about 15,000 people. The total population of the United States at independence was about 2.5 million, compared to about 320 million today.

THE THREE BRANCHES OF GOVERNMENT

LEGISLATIVE
(makes laws)

EXECUTIVE
(carries out laws)

JUDICIAL
(evaluates laws)

CHAPTER 2
KEEPING PEACE

A LONG HISTORY

Though the Bill of Rights took many ideas from the Virginia Declaration of Rights, the concept of individual liberty had been gaining momentum in England for decades. This idea would reach its summit in the founding documents of the United States of America.

Fast Fact

VIRGINIA DECLARATION OF RIGHTS

The Virginia Declaration of Rights, drafted in 1776 by George Mason, is considered the first modern constitutional protection of individual rights for citizens. It proclaimed the inherent rights of men, including the right to reform or abolish "inadequate" government. The Declaration influenced a number of later documents, including the US Declaration of Independence (1776), the US Bill of Rights (1789), and the French Revolution's Declaration of the Rights of Man and of the Citizen (1789). This image, of Gunston Hall, home of George Mason, was commemorated on a 3-cent stamp.

REJECTION OF MONARCHY

In order to understand the Second Amendment and its inclusion in the Bill of Rights, we must understand its origin and history. The roots of the Second Amendment are in the English Bill of Rights of 1689, which set limits on the power of the monarch. The idea of the common people having any say in their government was a radical one at the time. This bill meant that the monarch, while still having a great deal of power, did not have *absolute* power over an individual. Individuals had a right to some control over their home and property, and that property included firearms.

Fast Fact

KING WILLIAM III AND QUEEN MARY II

After nearly a half century of civil war in England, King James II was deposed. He was replaced by his daughter and her husband, who became King William and Queen Mary (shown here), in what was known as the Glorious Revolution of 1688. The resulting Bill of Rights is seen by many as significant for its restriction of power of the monarchy.

DECISION TIME

Most Colonial Americans supported these rights for individuals. However, when the Continental Congress voted for independence from England on July 2, 1776, Americans had to decide if they were willing to take up arms against King George III and the greatest power in the world at that time.

Many colonial men were required by law to own firearms in order to support their local militia. This law backfired on the Crown when those same arms were used in the revolution against the army of King George III.

Fast Fact

KING GEORGE III

The role of King George III in events leading up to the American Revolution has long been debated. Some argue that, as a constitutional monarch whose powers were limited by the Bill of Rights of 1689, George (pictured here) was not directing events but merely reacting to them. Others blame the king for imposing taxes, limiting the rights of colonists, and ignoring their pleas. Thomas Jefferson called him a "tyrant" and declared him "unfit" to rule.

FIREARMS

Across the 13 colonies, men from all social classes enlisted in the Continental Army. Right from the start, supplying this new army with proper weapons was a struggle because the new government had problems raising money for firearms and organizing their transport. As a result of these problems, many soldiers used their own firearms in battle, especially at the beginning of the war.

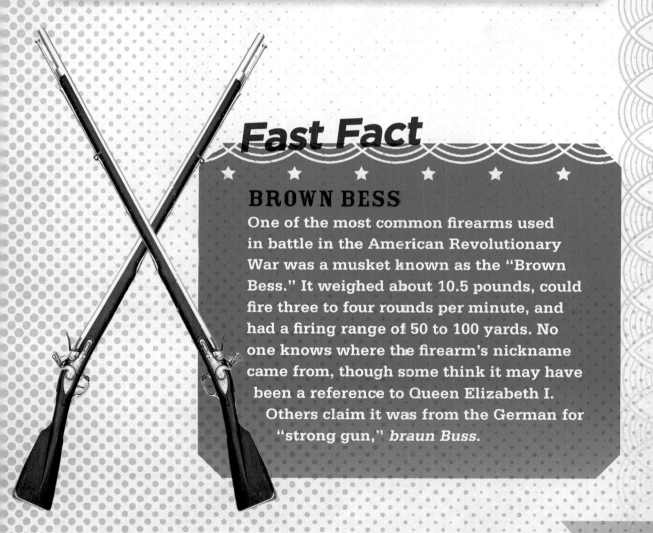

Fast Fact

BROWN BESS

One of the most common firearms used in battle in the American Revolutionary War was a musket known as the "Brown Bess." It weighed about 10.5 pounds, could fire three to four rounds per minute, and had a firing range of 50 to 100 yards. No one knows where the firearm's nickname came from, though some think it may have been a reference to Queen Elizabeth I. Others claim it was from the German for "strong gun," *braun Buss.*

DEFENSE OF LIBERTY

When the Revolutionary War was over, the government of the United States of America was on shaky ground. The leaders of the new nation wanted to prevent any kind of counterrevolution.

American citizens were exhausted and just wanted to live in peace. The question was how to go about keeping that peace. There was no standing army, and most people did not want one. They had finally gained their freedom, and standing armies represented to them the repression and intolerance they (or their ancestors) had experienced in Europe or colonial America.

The Founding Fathers feared that King George III would try to incite a counterrevolution in his former colonies. In 1789, the year of the French Revolution, Thomas Jefferson wrote to John Adams, then the US **ambassador** to Great Britain, "We I hope shall be left free to avail ourselves of the advantages of neutrality: and yet much I fear the English, or rather their stupid king, will force us out of it…"

Thomas Jefferson (1743–1826) was the main author of the Declaration of Independence (1776) and an advocate of democracy and republicanism.

MILITIAS AND DEFENSE

Because there was no standing army, most Americans owned firearms not just for their personal use, but in case they were called upon to defend their new country. The defense of the United States was now the job of irregular state militias, not the federal government. As people who had lived under more centralized systems for so long, this seemed a breath of fresh air to most Americans.

Much of the fighting in the American Revolution was carried out by colonial militias against the professional British army, as seen in this drawing of the Battle of Lexington, 1775.

INDIVIDUAL FREEDOM

While the new country was struggling to get its footing, the idea of individual gun ownership became deeply ingrained in the American mind. In the post-Revolutionary era, gun ownership was not just something people wanted, but something that most people *needed* in their everyday lives. Many lived in rural areas where legal authorities were not close at hand, and they had to defend their property when it was threatened by thieves or **poachers**. They also needed firearms to hunt for food. The thought of giving up their guns would have been laughable to them.

Fast Fact

DANIEL BOONE

Daniel Boone (1734–1820) was a renowned hunter, trapper, and explorer. He was one of America's first folk heroes. In the 1770s, he discovered a trail though the Cumberland Gap that he developed to allow settlers access to lands in Kentucky and the West. He also served as a militia captain, organizing the defense of the settlements along his route. He is rarely pictured without his trusty flintlock rifle.

GUN OWNERSHIP TODAY

Almost all Americans now live in a very different environment from the one that their Revolutionary ancestors knew. Even so, many still hold the same view of gun ownership. They believe that they are responsible enough to keep guns on their person and in their homes. They think that their ownership of firearms is none of the government's business. This leads to contentious interactions with Americans who disagree with them.

A woman fires a handgun at an indoor gun range.

CHAPTER 3

WAR OF WORDS

A MATTER OF CLARITY

Is the Second Amendment clear enough? There did not seem to be too much question about it when it was written, but in modern times, the arguments over it never seem to end.

Fast Fact

GUN SHOWS

About 5,000 gun shows, such as this one held in Winneconne, Wisconsin, in April 2016, are held every year in the United States. Unlike gun stores, which have Federal Firearms Licenses, private-party sellers at gun shows are not required by federal law to do background checks on buyers. However, some states have their own background check laws for private sales.

BOTH SIDES OF THE CASE

Although our attention spans seem to get shorter all the time, and we love to communicate in tweets that have only 140 characters, the Second Amendment still looks very brief to our twenty-first-century eyes: "A well-regulated militia being necessary to the security of a free state, the right of the people to keep and bear arms shall not be infringed." The problem is that its wording can be interpreted in several ways.

Some people think that being able to carry handguns is the American way. Others disagree.

WHO, WHAT, WHY?

The Second Amendment seems to blur the line between collective and individual gun ownership. Can individuals own guns for any reason at all, or only for some "good" reasons, or only for the sake of a "well-regulated militia"? Can they own as many as they want, or should there be limits enforced by the government? And should the authority that enforces those limits be the local, state, or federal government?

To try to answer these questions, we must look at the argument from both the conservative and liberal points of view. Remember that these points represent what conservatives and liberals *generally* believe and do not speak for all members of those groups.

LIBERAL

CONSERVATIVE

There are different views on every issue, and gun control and ownership is no exception.

THE CONSERVATIVE SIDE

Conservatives generally believe that the Second Amendment is as relevant today as the day it was written, and that a very simple subject is being unnecessarily complicated and overanalyzed. They argue that the Second Amendment speaks of individual gun ownership not only for the defense of one's country, but for personal use. The government has no right, they say, to tell individuals what they may or may not do with their firearms, as long as they obey the law and do not infringe the rights of others.

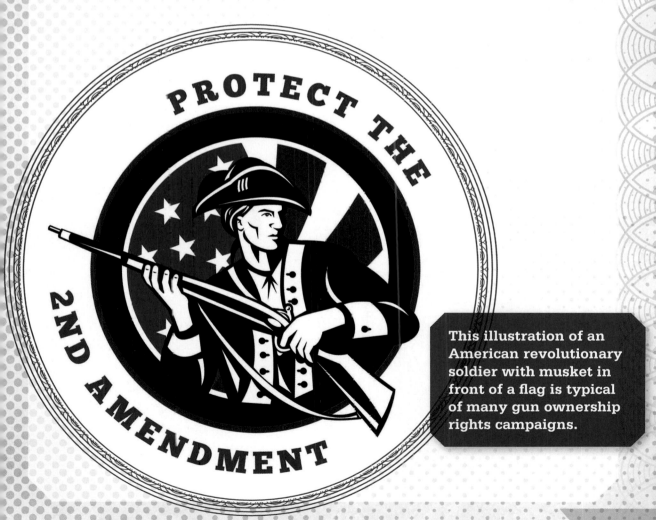

PROTECT THE 2ND AMENDMENT

This illustration of an American revolutionary soldier with musket in front of a flag is typical of many gun ownership rights campaigns.

NO RESTRICTIONS

Conservatives often argue that the number or types of guns a person owns should be irrelevant. If a person is not hurting others, what does it matter if he or she owns one gun or a hundred? Why is it the government's business how many guns people have? The types of guns they own should not matter, either, they say. Whether it is a handgun in a dresser drawer, a rifle used for hunting game, or an assault weapon for target shooting, what difference does it make? If a person is not committing any crimes, why should anyone, even the government, care? Many conservatives who believe strongly in these ideas belong to the National Rifle Association of America (NRA), a controversial group that lobbies Washington against gun control laws.

Fast Fact

THE NRA

The National Rifle Association of America (NRA) was founded on November 17, 1871. It claims more than 5 million members. As well as lobbying for lenient gun laws, the NRA places an emphasis on teaching adults and youths to handle firearms safely.

THE LIBERAL SIDE

Many liberals disagree with the conservative point of view about the Second Amendment, but there seems to be more of a spectrum of opinion on the liberal side. Some liberals believe that all guns not used in law enforcement should be banned. Other liberals believe that assault weapons should be banned, but that if someone needs a handgun for protection, or if they want to use a rifle for hunting purposes, that is acceptable.

Fast Fact

SHOOTINGS HORROR

Liberals often point to the horror of school shootings to bolster their arguments for strong gun control. But conservatives say that if well-armed "good guys" had been at those shootings, they could have prevented them or at least lessened the death tolls.

Teachers organize schoolchildren outdoors during an emergency.

FATAL SHOOTINGS

Wherever they are on this spectrum, most liberals think that the Second Amendment has been interpreted in damaging ways. They believe that anyone who wants to buy a firearm of any kind should be subjected to a thorough background check.

ORLANDO

On June 12, 2016, America saw its worst mass shooting in modern times. Conservatives believed this crime to be a case of radical Islamic terrorism and that it was the idea that should be fought, not the guns that were used. Liberals, on the other hand, believed this crime to be a case of homophobia, as most of the victims were gay people. Liberals believed that conservatives were trying to ignore the gay victims, and they called for stronger gun control as a way to protect the gay community and all Americans. Politicians on both sides heard the concerns of their constituents and used the media to get their views across to the public.

The murder of 49 people (and wounding of 53) at Pulse nightclub in Orlando, Florida, was the deadliest mass shooting in US history.

TIMES HAVE CHANGED

The liberal argument rests on the fact that more than two centuries have passed since the writing of the Bill of Rights. While human beings are still the same, the guns they use are not the same—nor is the environment in which guns are used. Liberals believe that these points should be taken into account when discussing the Second Amendment. Could our forefathers have possibly imagined a world in which a mentally ill person could walk into Sandy Hook Elementary School with a gun and kill 20 children and 6 adults, as one man did in Newtown, Connecticut in December 2012? Liberals say no.

Fast Fact

SCHOOL SHOOTINGS

On December 15, 2012, the day after the Sandy Hook school shooting in Newtown, Connecticut, Shannon Watts founded the anti-gun-violence group Moms Demand Action for Gun Sense in America. The group now has a membership of 130,000.

CHAPTER 4

DEBATE AND DECISIONS

YEARS OF CONSENSUS

For many years, there was little debate in America over the meaning of the Second Amendment. Most of the population was spread across rural, agricultural areas; the government was far less centralized than it is today. It just seemed like common sense for people to own their own firearms.

Fast Fact

URBANIZATION AND GUNS

The **Industrial Revolution** took place in the United States from about 1760 to around 1820 or 1840. It transformed the economy from agricultural to industrial and brought many citizens who had once lived in rural America into the cities. This changed the way people thought about guns and gun laws, because people were living closer together and had better access to law enforcement. It is increasingly difficult to hunt for your breakfast when you live in a city high-rise: there isn't much game in the neighborhood park!

CLARIFYING GUN OWNERSHIP

As the population gradually shifted to urban areas and the federal government became more powerful, the US court system was called upon to clarify the issue of gun ownership and the meaning of the Second Amendment.

LEVELS OF COURTS

The judicial branch of our government has three levels: federal, state, and local. Issues that cannot be resolved at the local level move up the judiciary until they reach the highest court in the land, the Supreme Court.

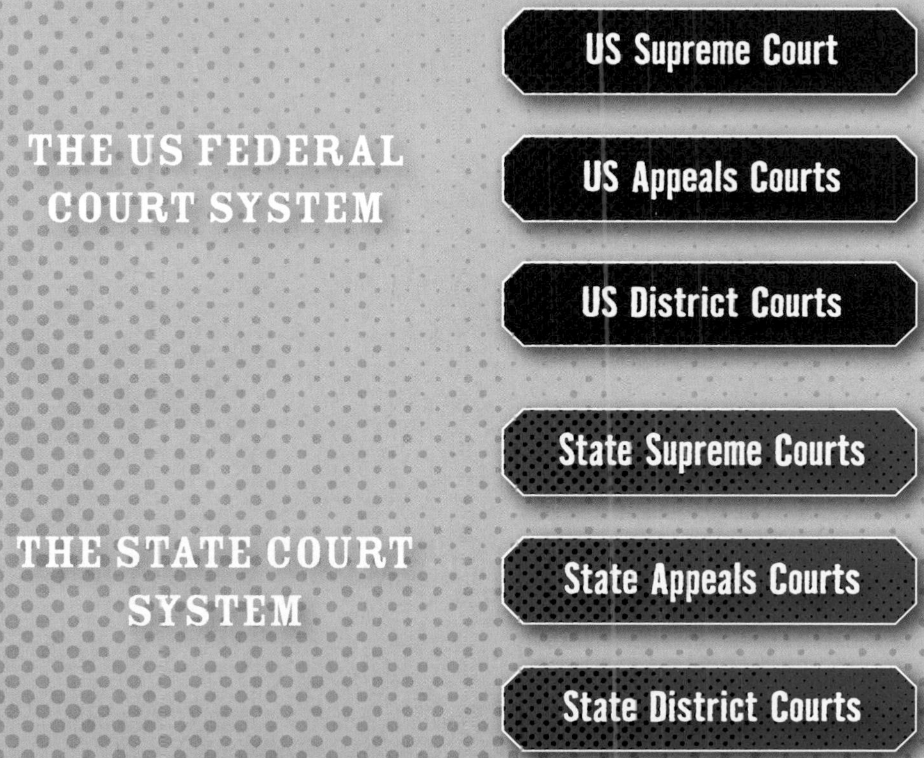

THE US FEDERAL COURT SYSTEM

US Supreme Court

US Appeals Courts

US District Courts

THE STATE COURT SYSTEM

State Supreme Courts

State Appeals Courts

State District Courts

THE COURTS WEIGH IN

The first Supreme Court case to affect the right to bear arms was *United States v. Cruikshank* in 1875. This case was the result of the Colfax Massacre of April 1873, when more than 100 black Republican freedmen were murdered by a mob of white Louisiana Democrats. Members of the white mob were arrested and charged. However, the courts dismissed the charges, and the Supreme Court agreed. The justices stated in their decision that "the right to bear arms is not granted by the Constitution; neither is it in any manner dependent upon that instrument for its existence." This has made their decision a popular one quoted by gun control supporters.

Then in 1886, in *Presser v. the People of Illinois*, the Supreme Court ruled that states could not disarm "all citizens capable of bearing arms" because the federal government had a right to a well-armed militia.

Fast Fact

APPOINTMENT FOR LIFE

Supreme Court justices are nominated by the president and confirmed by the Senate. Unlike the president, senators, and congressmen, Supreme Court justices have lifelong tenure, but some choose to retire. Since the court was established, there have been 112 justices, and fewer than half—just 54—have retired. The first justice to opt for retirement was John Jay, who was also the very first Supreme Court Chief Justice (1789–1795).

MILITIA GROUPS

The *Cruikshank* and *Presser* decisions clearly imply that the states can disarm *some* citizens, and that the protection of the federal government *might* be more important than personal liberty. The *Presser* ruling was limited, and regulated citizen militia groups. However, in 1939, the Court's decision in *United States v. Miller* stated that private individuals could own militia-type weapons, even if they were not members of a militia.

The *Miller* case challenged the National Firearms Act of 1934 in response to the St. Valentine's Day Massacre of 1929, which required the registration and taxing of all firearms.

Fast Fact

ST. VALENTINE'S DAY MASSACRE

At 10:30 on the morning of February 14, 1929, in a warehouse at 2122 North Clark Street in Chicago, seven gangsters, most of them members of George "Bugs" Moran's North Side Gang, were murdered. Moran, the main target of the attack, escaped death that day only because he decided to sleep in! Moran broke the gangster code of silence and publicly accused Al Capone (pictured here in 1930), leader of the rival South Side Gang, of the crime. No one was ever charged.

ASSAULT WEAPONS LEGAL

The *Miller* case has had far-reaching effects in the debate over gun ownership. Many gun control activists decry the use of assault weapons in mass shootings, but with gun rights organizations pointing to rulings such as the one in *Miller*, it would be very difficult—some argue impossible—to take these types of weapons away from law-abiding individuals.

Even the term "assault weapon" means different things to different people. A Federal Assault Weapons Ban was passed in 1994, banning the import or manufacture of certain semi-automatic weapons and magazines holding more than 10 rounds. The law expired in 2004. Repeated attempts to replace it have failed.

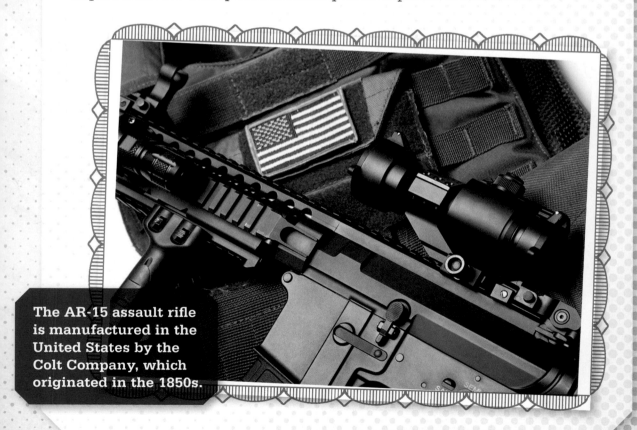

The AR-15 assault rifle is manufactured in the United States by the Colt Company, which originated in the 1850s.

FELONS AND FIREARMS

All was quiet on the Second Amendment front for decades, until the Supreme Court ruled in *Lewis v United States* (1980) to forbid the possession of firearms by the vast majority of convicted **felons**. Most American criminals who commit felonies can never own firearms again, but there are exceptions for some white-collar crimes and for those convicted in foreign countries. For felons who have been convicted of violent crimes, however, it is almost impossible to own a gun legally in the United States.

In most cases, it is illegal for convicted felons to own guns.

RESTORATION OF CIVIL RIGHTS

Convicted felons who want to own firearms must go through a process of having their civil rights restored. They must show ample evidence that they have reformed and have steady work and strong ties to their families and communities. Federal applications to the US Attorney General of the Bureau of Alcohol, Tobacco, and Firearms are often held up at this review stage. A competent, experienced **attorney** can make all the difference in having one's Second Amendment rights restored.

Fast Fact

CHICAGO GUN BAN

Chicago has battled the court system in an effort to keep the sale of handguns illegal. When the Supreme Court ruled against the city in 2010, the city responded by placing the strictest laws on gun sales that it could, forcing sellers to video-record sales and restricting buyers to one firearm purchase per month.

GUN RULINGS

In 1990, in *United States v. Verdugo-Urquidez*, the Supreme Court declared that "the people" in the Second Amendment were those who had "developed sufficient connection with this country to be considered part of that community." This ruling is often cited by pro-gun rights activists as proof that the Second Amendment guarantees firearm rights to individuals. In its decision in *District of Columbia v. Heller* in 2008, the Supreme Court ruled that the Second Amendment protects an individual's right to own a gun for lawful use such as self-defense. And in 2010, in *McDonald v. Chicago*, the Supreme Court invalidated Chicago's handgun ban and ruled that the Second Amendment applied to states.

While *McDonald* is the most recent Supreme Court case regarding the Second Amendment, it was a 5–4 split decision, and it is unlikely to be the last word on the subject.

The Second Amendment allows Americans to own guns for self-defense.

CHAPTER 5

THE NEVER-ENDING BATTLE

CONTINUING CONTROVERSY

The battle over the Second Amendment in the United States shows no sign of ending. But why? And what can be done about it?

GOOD-GUY THEORY

Even after a seemingly endless parade of mass shootings in workplaces and schools, gun rights advocates continue to insist that individuals are safer when armed, and that belief will not change anytime soon. Such advocates typically contend that mass shootings either would not happen or would take fewer lives if "good guys" on the scene were armed. They point to cases in which their "good-guy" theory appears to be right.

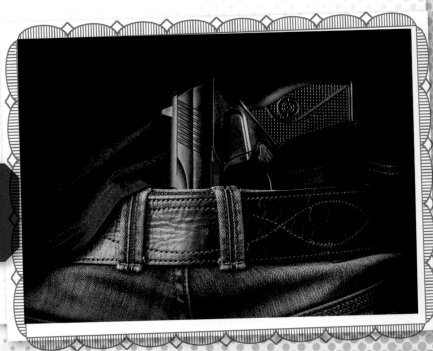

Some people think that a "good guy" carrying a gun can stop a "bad guy" with a gun.

STOPPING THE BAD GUY

On October 1, 1997, Luke Woodham walked into his high school in Pearl, Mississippi, and used a firearm to kill two students and injure sever. more. Woodham then tried to walk across the street to kill more students at a middle school, but assistant principal Joel Myrick took a semi-automatic pistol from his truck and detained him until authorities arrived.

RETURNING FIRE

In 2014, Richard Plotts shot and killed a caseworker at Mercy Fitzgerald Hospital near Philadelphia. He then shot and wounded his psychiatrist, Lee Silverman. But Silverman pulled his own gun from his pocket and started shooting back, wounding Plotts and holding him until police could arrive. Plotts had 39 more rounds of **ammunition** on him, and authorities said they believed he would have used them.

ARMED RESPONSE

In another case, Abraham Dicken went into an AT&T store in New York Mills, New York, on May 27, 2010, with a .357 magnum and a list of people he wanted to kill. An off-duty police officer, Donald J. Moore, used his personal firearm to shoot and kill Dicken, who had already injured one employee. Gun rights advocates argue that the death toll that day would have been much higher had Moore not been there with his weapon.

Fast Fact

THE .357 MAGNUM

The .357 Magnum (such as the one pictured here) is a revolver cartridge developed by the Smith & Wesson and Winchester companies in the 1930s. General George S. Patton carried two ivory-handled revolvers, one of which was a Smith & Wesson .357 Magnum. Patton bought the gun in October 1935 and had the original walnut grips replaced with ivory in 1940.

MENTAL HEALTH TREATMENT

Second Amendment supporters sometimes promote the idea that better treatment for the mentally ill is a more effective solution to gun violence than the confiscation of firearms from law-abiding people.

Fast Fact

MENTAL ILLNESS

It is estimated that some 42.5 million American adults experience some form of mental illness every year. Many people assume that mental health problems and violence are strongly connected, but doctors and researchers at Harvard Medical School report that "most individuals with psychiatric disorders are not violent."

BUT ON THE OTHER HAND...

Anti-gun advocates say that while the Mississippi and New York cases support the "good-guy" theory at first glance, with deeper investigation, they prove to be exceptions to the rule. Yes, Joel Myrick stopped Luke Woodham from entering another school, but Myrick was a US Army Reserve commander who was trained in the proper use of firearms. Likewise, Donald J. Moore was a law enforcement agent, someone who can be trusted to use good judgment in such situations.

Military personnel and law enforcement officials receive firearms training.

HOW FRIENDLY?

Should just *anyone* be able to carry a firearm and take the law into their own hands when a tragedy occurs? What if they are not properly trained? What if innocent bystanders are hit by "**friendly fire**"? And when law enforcement officers arrive on the scene, how are they supposed to tell the good guy with a gun from the bad guy with a gun?

Fast Fact

BACKFIRE

On May 2, 2016, Ricci Bradden shot and wounded his wife in the parking lot of a drugstore. After witnessing the altercation, Anthony Antell Jr., a retired marine and father of three, grabbed a gun from his car and confronted Bradden. But the heroic rescue attempt went wrong when Bradden slapped the gun out of Antell's hand and shot him, killing him.

FIREARMS AND SAFETY

Those working for stronger gun laws continue to point to scientific evidence they say proves that people are safer, overall, when they do not own or use firearms. A study conducted in October 2013, in which researchers analyzed data from 27 countries, came to the conclusion that there is a very strong correlation between the number of guns people own and the number of deaths resulting from firearms. Previous studies have shown the same link.

ACCIDENTS

In the year 2015 alone, at least 265 children accidentally shot themselves or others after finding unsecured guns, and 83 of those shootings were fatal. Anti-gun activists say that this is more than enough proof that firearm laws should be much stricter than they are now. They want the American people to look at the big picture rather than just a few stories of heroes racing in to save the day.

THE AMERICAN WAY

The debate over the right to bear arms may never be settled in the United States. The Bill of Rights and its inclusion of the Second Amendment are food for thought, not only for constitutional scholars, but to all of us who call this nation home. While the continuing argument can be seen as a sign of disunity among America's citizens, it is also a reassuring demonstration of democracy at work.

The debate over the Second Amendment and guns will probably go on for a very long time.

GLOSSARY

abolitionism—the movement to end the enslavement of African Americans

ambassador—someone sent to another country as a representative of their own country

amendment—an alteration or addition to a bill

ammunition—material, such as bullets, that is fired from a gun

Anti-Federalist—an opponent of a centralized, federal government

attorney—a lawyer; a legal representative

felon—a criminal who has committed a serious crime (called a felony)

friendly fire—gunfire that harms those on the same side of a battle

Industrial Revolution—the replacement of hand tools with power machines

militia—a body of citizens enrolled for on-and-off military duty

monarchy—a country that is ruled by a monarch (such as a king or queen)

poacher—someone who trespasses on private property for the purpose of stealing livestock

ratify—to give legal or official approval

FURTHER INFORMATION

Books

Cook, Philip J. and Kristin A. Goss. *The Gun Debate: What Everyone Needs to Know*. New York: Oxford University Press, 2014.

Halbrook, Stephen P. *The Founders' Second Amendment: Origins of the Right to Bear Arms*. Lanham, MD: Ivan R. Dee, 2012.

Waldman, Michael. *The Second Amendment: A Biography*. New York: Simon & Schuster, 2014.

Winkler, Adam. *Gun Fight: The Battle Over the Right to Bear Arms in America*. New York: W.W. Norton & Co., 2011.

Online

Cornell University Law School/Legal Information Institute
www.law.cornell.edu/wex/second_amendment

Gun Ownership and Firearm Related Deaths Study
www.ncbi.nlm.nih.gov/pubmed/24054955

Harvard Medical School: Mental Health and Violence
www.health.harvard.edu/newsletter_article/mental-illness-and-violence

International Business Times: Accidental Gun Deaths Are a Major Problem in the US
www.ibtimes.com/accidental-gun-deaths-involving-children-are-major-problem-us-2250568

National Constitution Center
constitutioncenter.org/interactive-constitution/amendments/amendment-ii

INDEX